Grace ✳ ✳ for ✳ ✳ President!

Becky Manfredini and Jenny Reznick

Illustrated by KE Lewis

Rigby
A Harcourt Achieve Imprint

www.Rigby.com
1-800-531-5015

Scene 1: A Classroom

NARRATOR: It is three days before the student council election. Steven is helping Grace with her speech. Their helpers are making posters.

GRACE: My fellow students, please vote for student council president on Friday. My advice is this: Choose me, Grace Molina. I will do a good job and work hard.

STEVEN: That's a great start! I think people will really like your ideas.

GRACE: Thanks! I want them to know that I can be a strong leader and a good listener.

HELPER #1: Grace, you need a slogan on your posters.

HELPER #2: We like "Take our advice, Grace is nice."

HELPER #1: How about "Vote for Grace in the council race"?

GRACE: I like them both. Let's put them together.

HELPER #2: I think we should put them on all our posters.

STEVEN: Yes, we need lots and lots of posters.

NARRATOR: The next day, Steven asks students who they plan to vote for. Later at lunch, Steven plans to tell Grace what he learns.

Today is Wednesday, September 20
Remember FRIDAY is
Election Day!!

STEVEN: Grace, half of the kids will vote for you, but half might vote for Ben Marks. I think we need to make a lot more posters.

GRACE: Ben has a lot of good ideas for the student council. This is going to be a hard race to win.

BEN: Hi, Grace. Hi, Steven. I can't wait until we give our speeches Thursday.

GRACE: I'm excited, too.

BEN: Good luck, Grace. May the best person win!

GRACE: I need a new idea.

STEVEN: A new poster?

GRACE: No, I need to do
something that students care
about. But what?

NARRATOR: Later that day, Grace goes to her P.E. class. Grace notices something about the balls and jump ropes.

GRACE: All the equipment is old and worn out. We can't play any sports! This stuff needs to be replaced.

GRACE: Coach Sikes, why is all of our gym stuff worn out?

COACH SIKES: Well, Grace, I'm not sure anyone notices but you and me. Somebody needs to tell the principal that we need new equipment.

GRACE: Who can convince the school to buy new basketballs and jump ropes?

COACH SIKES: That sounds like a job for the student council.

GRACE: Coach Sikes, you just gave me an idea!

15

Scene 4: A Phone Call

NARRATOR: That night Grace calls Steven on the phone.

GRACE: Steven, I found something I can do to stand out. I know what will make people vote for me!

STEVEN: What is it? Do we need to make a new poster?

GRACE: Never mind the posters, Steven. I have a great idea.

STEVEN: Well, what is it?

GRACE: You'll hear it tomorrow.

NARRATOR: It is Thursday. A large crowd comes to hear Ben and Grace give their speeches.

BEN: My name is Ben Marks. I am running for student council president. I promise to do a good job. I will work hard for everyone. Thank you.

NARRATOR: Grace speaks next.

GRACE: I'm Grace Molina. Have you noticed that our P.E. equipment is old and broken? I will work to get new P.E. equipment. I'll also look for ways to make our school even better. Thank you.

NARRATOR: On Friday all the students go to the gym to vote. Grace votes, too.

GRACE: I hope people like my ideas to help the school.

NARRATOR: Grace can hardly wait to find out who won.

GRACE: I wonder when they will announce the winner. Do you think I will win?

STEVEN: Oh, yes. We hung up a lot of posters.

NARRATOR: Friday afternoon an announcement is made. All the votes have been counted. Grace is very nervous as she listens to the results.

STUDENT REPORTER: And the new president is...

STUDENT REPORTER: Grace Molina!

NARRATOR: Everyone cheers. Ben congratulates Grace.

BEN: Good luck, President Grace.

GRACE: Thanks, Ben!